# FIRST STEPS

## Other books by William Bloom

*Devas, Fairies and Angels*

*Meditation in a Changing World —*
*An Introduction to Individual and Group Meditation*

*The Sacred Magician*

*Sacred Times — A New Approach to Festivals*

*The New Age* (editor)

*The Seeker's Guide* (edited with John Button)

# FIRST STEPS

## An Introduction to Spiritual Practice

William Bloom

Findhorn Press

British Library Cataloguing-in-Publication Data.
A catalogue record for this book is available
from the British Library.


Set in Palatino by Findhorn Press
Cover design by Ronald Morton
Author photograph by Elke Heyer
Printed and bound by The Cromwell Press, Melksham, England

Published by Findhorn Press, The Park, Findhorn,
Forres IV36 0TZ, Scotland

*For Allen Gold*

# Contents

# Chapter One

# The Basics

## A Human-Centred Approach

Starting off on the path of self-discovery and of spiritual exploration is not easy. There appear to be too many choices, too many opportunities for delusion and error. It is not so difficult for people who feel comfortable within the embrace of a particular religious tradition, for that tradition will provide clear guidelines for spiritual exploration. But many people today are not at ease within a particular discipline or school. They want to learn about the basic principles which all the spiritual traditions have in common and to make their own decisions about spiritual practice.

This short book is for people who have begun to explore spiritual realities and who need an introduction to the general principles and features of spiritual practice:

- How to explore the inner world of the self.
- How to explore the inner world of all life.
- How to integrate this exploration and make it relevant to everyday living.

The challenge then is to achieve clarity about these basic principles. That is the purpose of *First Steps*. I have tried to extract the essence of the teachings from the different traditions and to present them simply, using a psychological approach. For whether we are eighteen or eighty, western city dweller or rural farmer, woman or man, we share a common psychology: we are all human.

I hope that I have succeeded in identifying these common features of spiritual practice and that all of the varying traditions feel themselves properly represented here. But if you feel comfortable in one tradition, then I have no inclination at all to pull you away from it. The tradition into which you were born may be perfect for you; it might be stupid to ignore it. I know one woman, for example, who has made a successful career publishing books about all the different paths, but who has carefully remained within the Christian tradition, using the established maps of the Church to guide her spiritual practice. My own history, on the other hand, has been more varied. Coming from an agnostic background with parents who were suspicious of religion in general, I have found useful guidance and fundamental insights in the Sufi, Tibetan Buddhist, Christian Gnostic and Western Mystery traditions; and I recognise and honour the wisdom and heritage of all the other paths, great and small.

A psychological, or human-centred, approach is also useful because it avoids theological prisons for the mind and spirit. What I try to share in this book are the basic methods for exploring inner reality. If I describe them well and accurately, then whatever your intellectual or religious background they should ring true and feel appropriate. If they do not, ignore them. In the final analysis each of us has to discover, or uncover, our own approach and experience.

Nor is it my purpose to teach specific forms and techniques. I want to help readers understand the basic dynamics and also, hopefully, encourage you to put them into practice. You can then choose to use the help of a particular path; or you can choose to work following your own sense and intuition.

## Resumé

The basic message of *First Steps* is that spiritual practice consists of three interwoven dynamics:

Every day, in some way

- We review, contemplate and transform our attitudes and actions.
- We align with and explore the inner and sacred dimensions of self and life.
- We serve.

Perfectly, all three happen simultaneously and continuously. They also need to happen

- With a general attitude of amused realism about our relative state of ignorance, and
- With an interest in seeking continuing education and inspiration.

In the following chapters, then, I first look at the innate seeds of spirituality within all of us and at the challenges of being human, and then I go on to describe in greater detail the basic dynamics of spiritual practice.

Chapter Two

# The Inner World,
# the Sacred and Morality

## The Three Seeds

Many of us think that we are not spiritual, and when circumstances unfold so that we begin to approach spiritual realities, we do so with some suspicion. We are suspicious perhaps that some religion or spiritual teacher is going to try to catch us and limit and manipulate our search. We are also suspicious because we think that we are so far away from spiritual and inner realities that they are actually beyond our reach.

I think it is appropriate to be suspicious of institutions and teachers. I do not think it is appropriate to be suspicious of our own innate connection with the sacred and the multidimensional. It is in all of us, if only we would notice it.

Each of us in our own unique way has, from childhood, the following innate senses:

- A sense of an inner life and an inner self.
- A sense of the sacred.
- A sense of morality and natural justice.

These are seeds within us to be loved and cultivated.

## The Inner World and Inner Self

As children, we each of us had a secret inner sense that we were special. We were not simply the children seen by the adults around us; we were heroines and heroes of our own inner and mythic worlds. We lived naturally in two worlds simultaneously, the outer and the inner, and the two fused and intertwined in our experience, play and imagination. Our consciousness lived in a reality both seen and unseen.

As we grew up, however, the harsh realities of life inevitably intruded into our consciousness, sometimes slowly, sometimes cruelly and abruptly, and the inner world — such stuff as dreams are made of — retreated. It did not evaporate, but it became hidden beneath layers of psychological defence. These defences are attitudes and moods that we have built up so that we can function in the real world.

We were all children once who lived in an unbounded reality and who then, in the face of the harsh realities of life, suppressed this inner cosmos. At some point, later in our life, triggered by one of a kaleidoscope of possible causes, we begin to feel a need to return to this inner life. Sometimes we are confused by this instinct, which may seem naive and childish. Some of us may even feel ashamed.

Of course, it is not possible to return to be the children who we were. Time has passed and we have changed. The confusion or shame which some of us experience as we reawaken is a confusion based in a simple mistake. There is no need to recover our childhood. There is only a need to recover the consciousness that childhood allowed us, that access to the inner world. We need to recover the inner world, not as the children we were, but as the people we are now — perhaps cynical, aggressive and frigid; perhaps analytical, ambitious and bitter; perhaps generous and wise. Whoever we are, whatever we have become, there still comes the urge to rediscover and explore the other dimensions of our psyche.

There is no point in regretting that we did not hold on to our inner lives and begin the great inner voyage of discovery as children. If we had launched ourselves into explorations of the inner world then, how wisely would we have pursued our search? Who would have been there to support and help us? Perhaps the realities and insights would anyway have been too profound, too relentless, too ecstatic, too tragic for us to have been able to cope with them.

## The Sacred

Many people think that they have never had, and never will have, a mystical experience. And it is true that many of us may never have that classic mystic experience of dissolving ecstatically into the unity of the universe. But there are other levels of experience.

The imaginative perceptions of children are not simply internal, but also relate to the outside world. The inner imaginative magic is in relationship with an outer magic. We easily see figures and beings in clouds or in flames. We stand in the forest and are caught by the mysteries of the shadows and the presence of the trees. When someone kind and thoughtful enters our life we experience a direct glow of warmth and affection. And there are times, perhaps looking at the sky or imagining the whole solar system as an atom in our fingernail, when we know that there is a magic to the whole of life.

Our young minds may also seek to understand infinity. Where does space end? What is on the other side? In all of these experiences we get caught in a transcendent consciousness. It is bigger than us, too huge to understand, wonderful and sacred.

We all have tastes of sacred experience. As children we had easier access to these experiences, but we took them for granted, forgot them as we grew older and they became layered with adult realities.

Knowing that life is sacred — from the galaxy down to the tiniest flower — is not a heavy religious or philosophical consideration. It is simple and lovely. Some mystics live continuously in this experience. We need only remember this sense of the magic and the sacred and recognise that, yes, we too have mystical experiences.

## Morality and Natural Justice

But it is not only the interior and sacred world of the inner child which echoes through our lives. There are other senses and intimations that haunt our minds and our hearts. The inner world of childhood is not a closed cosmos which ignores the here-and-now and is oblivious to daily realities. It has another distinct feature which fuels the deepest dynamics of human morality.

Although many cynics will deny it, we all carry deep within our psyche a sense of what is fair and just, of what is and what is not right behaviour. We do terrible and selfish things, but it does not mean that this sense of morality and justice does not exist. It means only that we ignore it. In fact, often we justify our own bad behaviour with the excuse that the situation was not fair. Even in our criminality we have a sense — albeit perverse — of justice. We may behave in cunning, spiteful and selfish ways, but whispering in our consciousness is an awareness of how the situation might also be.

For many of us, this sense of morality and natural justice becomes overwhelming and finally we know that we need to live our lives according to it. This realisation may come slowly or it may come stabbing the heart. In one of the European mystical traditions, the Rosicrucian, there is an image of a pelican feeding her young from the flesh of her own breast. This image is not one of meaningless self-sacrifice, but represents the deepest willingness that we have to serve and to bring about a life of natural justice. This instinct within us to do good wrestles with that other less altruistic one — the instinct to survive and to succeed in a threatening world. But of that struggle, more later.


## We Have Unique Paths

We each of us, then, possess these three seeds: knowing there is an inner life; a sense of the sacred; a sense of morality and natural justice.

But these are only seeds. The purpose of spiritual practice is to bring them to their full and unique potential. We need to avoid the trap of assuming that when each of us has brought those seeds to their full potential, we shall all then be the same. We each have our own unique psychological history, our own unique identity and personality. I am unlike Mother Teresa not just because I am a man. I am unlike her, or Jesus, or Buddha, because I am me.

Once, in meditation, I was contemplating what I would be like when perfect. I had been playing with images of the famous mystic teachers, founders of religions and saviours — the Great and Holy Ones. Suddenly they melted away and I was left simply with an experience of ME, everything I already knew, but perfectly fulfilled. It was an amusing, sobering and integrating experience. I had a taste of my full potential, my consciousness free of hooks. It was exhilarating. But simultaneously I was still everything I had always been. I had transformed into me, not into someone else. This is true for each of us. All we can turn into is ourselves.

# Chapter Three

# The Psychological Obstacles or the Layers of the Onion

## Switching On the Bullshit Antennae

Much of my life is spent with people who are consciously on the path of spiritual transformation. I work both with people who are apparently taking their first steps and with people who are spiritual teachers. And if there is one mistake that we all tend to make, it is to underestimate the psychological difficulties that are unavoidably ours.

If these problems are not acknowledged realistically at the very beginning of our spiritual journey, then the basic attitude with which we approach our transformation and service will be fundamentally off balance from the very beginning. If our initial attitude is naive, then we are bound to create difficulties, delusions and denials at the core of our spiritual practice. This issue requires special attention as many of us are reluctant to grasp the nettle of psychological reality. In fact, one of the healthy reasons why many people are suspicious of spirituality is precisely because people who are 'into spirituality' can be so naive about the reality of the human condition.

At the very beginning of the path we need to switch on our bullshit antennae. Attached to our head we have two invisible radar dishes which continuously rotate, scanning for illusions both inside and outside ourself.

## Primal Vulnerability

Let us look at the human condition and focus first on the hard reality of the newly born human infant.

The energy around birth is tremendous but at its core is an exhausted mother and a tiny, vulnerable creature. Leave the creature alone and it will cry and then die. This total vulnerability endures for several years and even when a certain physical self-reliance is possible, we are still poignantly vulnerable. There are no perfect parents, nor a perfect education system, nor a perfect culture or society. We are born with the biological instinct and need to survive physically. We then develop the core psychological instinct and need for a sense of self and identity. These two core needs, the physical and the psychological, are continuously confronted, battered and energetically affected by a cruel world. Human beings, all of us, are vulnerable and wounded. We all suffer the same condition.

But there is another side to that coin which also demands immediate recognition. One of our glories is our ability not simply to survive and cope, but to act and to create heroically. We are all great life artists. We are all natural adventurers. We need the breast, but we also need freedom. We need comfort, but we also seek challenge.

In order to survive and to cope, we build up layers of armour and defence, for how could we possibly live if we remained as open as we were as infants? The primal state of vulnerability is too raw for any of us to survive without protection. Twentieth-century psychological theory, beginning with the insights of Freud, clearly explains and illustrates the many dynamics involved in the creation of our wounds and the creation of the armour by which we defend ourselves. Wounding and armour are unavoidable.

There is, then, this spectrum of human behaviour —

from coping to acting heroically. In between the two, we create our cultures and societies. And all of this happens on top of our vulnerability and our psychological wounds.

## An Attitude of Realism

The path of spiritual transformation and service begins surely with an acknowledgement of the human condition. Knowing and accepting is a key attitude. Nothing about ourselves should be unacceptable. Every dark, unpleasant, cunning, ugly and pathological aspect of ourselves is acceptable to us. If we cannot accept it, then we will never be able to transform it. If there are aspects of ourselves that we cannot accept and therefore cannot transform, then our whole process of spiritual exploration and transformation is flawed from the very beginning.

With an attitude of knowing and accepting we can dare to have the courage to learn everything about ourselves. That apocryphal slogan over the entrance to the Temple at Delphi, *Know Thyself,* is far deeper, more complex and more paradoxical than the usual interpretation which suggests that it is encouraging us to know our true Self, the soul. In fact, it encourages us to know everything about ourselves — light and darkest shadow. We can only achieve this with an attitude of complete and realistic acceptance of what it is to be human.

Of all spiritual cultures, the Tibetan Buddhist is perhaps the most accepting of the realities of the human condition, which it regards with a wonderful sense of humour and compassionate detachment. Yes, a Tibetan Buddhist smiles, of course there is terrible suffering. It is very painful — grin, grin.

Look at the great religious paintings of the Buddhist

tradition and notice the serene meditator surrounded by terrible dragons, demons and monsters. The demons do not, as is often thought, represent the outside world impinging upon the pure practice of the meditator. These demons are all the shadow aspects of the meditator him- or herself. Nothing is denied. There is a wonderful Buddhist meditation which begins with the acknowledgement: *My body is a sack of skin full of unattractive things.* The meditator then goes on to list his organs as if in a butcher's shop.

The beauty of this approach is not just that it recognises these realities, but that the essential attitude is one of detachment, amusement and an eagerness to engage with the truth of our condition.

Yes, there is suffering. Yes, it hurts. But what is our attitude to the pain? We can whinge, moan and cry over spilt milk. We can be sensitive, sentimental and overwhelmed by it. We can, of course, try denying it — with a great big spiritual smile and naive angelic halo. Or we can, nodding with detached but understanding amusement, accept it.

In accepting the human condition, we can also begin to learn about compassion. And compassion begins not with looking at other people's problems but with accepting the realities of our own psychological state.


## A Particularly Cunning Layer of the Psychological Onion

A particularly cunning aspect of our psychology is that part of ourself that thinks it knows who we are. We need to recognise that who we think we are and the way in which we think about who we are, are conditioned by the culture in which we have been raised. This is obvious if we look at nationalism and religion. The same baby born and brought up in different places will have very different beliefs.

It is obvious — but just because it is obvious does not mean that we realise and accept it about ourselves.

I have looked at myself and I have had to presume that every thought and attitude I possess is the creation of the culture in which I have been brought up. Look at the rug that I can pull out from under my feet. My political attitudes of social justice reflect those of my parents. My sense of religious freedom reflects western European liberalism. My pick-and-choose approach to spiritual practice reflects my 60s flower-power background. All my friends have turned green and, for social and psychological comfort, I too have become ecologically aware.

It is possible for me to see myself as nothing more than the result of my culture. I wear no clothes that belong to me. I am clothed by everything around me. I am nothing but a social identity. We are all of us caught in the trap of how culture has taught us to feel and think.

Perhaps we do not even have the freedom to think ourselves out of it; because all our thought processes are modes internalised from our culture.

I become giddy, like a snake swallowing its own tail, as I attempt to think my way through all this.

The solution is detached realism. Accept the paradox of the social self who feels so real. This is just another layer of ourself about which we need to be aware, another layer of defence which has helped us survive and function.

So is there nothing about our identity onto which we can safely hold? I do not think so, and I do not think it a good idea that we should want to be certain about who we are.

Let us also be realistic in another way. Most of us possess personalities and identities that are certainly not blown away by the first gust of self-doubt. Most of us, in fact, require a form of psychic demolition before we even begin to face the truth about ourselves. I have experienced situations in which friends have queued up to show me the error of my ways and to point out a personality defect that required transforming. I have been told about it month after month, year after year. I have confidently ignored them. Years later I have finally been able to acknowledge that they were right.

There is another of these strange human paradoxes here. We are wounded and we put on layers of defence because we are so primally vulnerable. Yet, once the layers have been put on, they possess the staying power of reinforced concrete. Some of my personality defects are like the pyramids in Egypt: battered, no longer functioning, but — by Jove! — still there.

We need to trust nothing and to be prepared to accept any truth about ourselves. This is an attitude of wisdom. It is the safest place from which to start spiritual practice. This attitude of realism about ourselves is humbling in the best possible way.

The world of spiritual seekers, however, is scattered with eager disciples and teachers who glow with spiritual enthusiasm and charisma, but who are flawed and lack realism about themselves. There is tragedy in this ignorance.

The best possible psychological strategy is sincerely and joyfully to expect the very worst of oneself. This is sensible because it means we are open to anything. It creates a wide psychological space in which we have room to manoeuvre.


## Melting the Armour, Expanding Consciousness

You can see, therefore, that whatever else is needed for spiritual practice, we have to come to terms with our wounds and defences. They have to be healed and transformed. Left alone, they hinder our ability to expand our consciousness with clarity and they prevent us growing into who we really are.

There are two simultaneous pieces of psychological work that we do, then, in spiritual practice, which when flowing well can create a benevolent cycle. This benevolent cycle works like this:

- We expand our awareness to access new realities and dimensions. The new realities transform us.
- In being transformed, we melt through armour and through veils of illusion. Their melting allows us to expand our awareness even further.
- As we expand our awareness even further and as we allow the new consciousness to settle into our whole being, so the wounds and defences melt even more.

|  |  |
|---|---|
| New awareness | Melts armour |
| New energies | Heal wounds |

Some readers may have trouble believing that such a benevolent cycle exists. It may sound too positive and idealistic. Only practice will prove its truth. Surely, though, it is comforting to know that throughout the ages, in all spiritual traditions, seekers have reported that God — All That Is — is in essence love and compassion.

# Chapter Four

# Who Is the I?

*There once was a man who said, 'Though*
*I think that I know that I know,*
*I wish I could see*
*The I that knows me*
*When I know that I know that I know.*
(Alan Watts)

## Not Me, But I

This attitude of 'I am, but I am not what I think I am' is obviously not an easy one to adopt. It challenges us to understand ourselves in a completely new way. This new way must be so new that it does not even use our habitual mode of thinking. The idea is initially disorienting. In the Zen tradition there is a teaching method in which the teacher introduces the student to a paradox where the usual mode of thought and conceptualisation is irrelevant. When the student grasps this new mode of awareness, she is in Zen. The most famous illustration of this approach is the concept of one hand clapping.

Some eastern gurus were famous for telling their would-be disciples to dig a large hole in the ground, perhaps ten foot deep and ten foot square. The disciple labours hard, learning patience and endurance. At last:

'My hole is finished, Master.'

'Good,' comes the reply, 'now fill it in.'

R.D. Laing, the radical psychiatrist, sometimes used a similar approach. He told how he might deal with a patient. With great sincerity and warmth in his voice, and leaning sympathetically forward, he says to his patient:

'I love you. Because I love you, I can tell you the truth.'

He pauses.

'No one loves you.'

As we come to appreciate this attitude of detachment from who I think I am, we begin to be aware of some interesting questions concerning the nature of personal identity. If I am not this socio-psychological construct, who am I? In asking this question of ourselves, we are assuming that there is an I who is more than or different from who we thought we were. There is a new I to discover.

Spiritual practice is about discovering and exploring this new I. Spiritual practice is about becoming this I.

## The Core Self

The different religions, spiritual paths and belief systems say different things about the I. There are not only different names for it: soul, spirit, psyche, inner self, higher self, core self, multidimensional self. There are also different ideas about it.

Where there is agreement between the different belief systems is in the idea that the I is the major organising principle of who we are. Behind the psychological scenes the core self takes us forward through our life with a consistent and coherent dynamic. How this dynamic manifests varies from person to person. It is usual to accept that the core self organises our life so as to help us fulfil our true potential. And it is further assumed that to fulfil our true potential means becoming wiser, more integrated and more loving.

Why the core self does this and what the core self does after death and before birth is a subject of much discussion. The options include:

- The core self is a complex part of the biological mechanism of the human being and, at death, disintegrates in the same way as the physical body.
- The core self reincarnates, life by life building up a wiser, more integrated and loving identity, until finally it either dissolves in bliss or becomes a transcendent and eternal liberated consciousness.
- The core self is a peak in the vast ocean of the collective unconscious of humanity, finally dissolving back into that unconscious, but also serving to evolve and transform the totality.

Only you the individual, in the privacy of your own senses and intuitions, can decide about its true nature.

# Chapter Five

# Daily Self-Reflection

## The Two Selves

We are all faced with an inspiring, but irritating, challenge. We have this inspiring sense of our true inner self and we have the irritation of not being able to express it fully. This is a terrible paradox, isn't it? What greater frustration can there be for a human than to be told: this is who you really are — and you cannot be it; you can become it, but you are going to have to work at it.

But there is an even greater discomfort if, having become aware of our core self, we then ignore it.

There are two simultaneous pieces of work to do:

- First, we have to melt and transform the layers of our defences and daily attitudes.
- Second, we have to give attention to our core self and bring it more fully into our consciousness and actions.

'Self-reflection', then, is reflection on both the everyday personality self and on the inner Self.

## Reviewing the Personality Self

The basic principle of self-review is that by shining the light of awareness onto our attitudes and behaviour we can begin to transform them; and as we transform them, this allows who we truly are to become more present. There are many techniques for doing this, but I think they can be usefully summarised in three basic approaches:

- Contemplative review.
- Journal-keeping.
- Breath.

Whichever technique we use — and all three can be combined — they need to be based in as much self-honesty as we can achieve. Over the years, as we practise self-review, the ability to look frankly at our dark apects increases. This is work that we do on our own. In the privacy of our own reflection we can be absolutely honest with ourselves. It is not worth being anything less. In the Christian tradition this form of self-reflection has been externalised into Confession, in which the honesty occurs in a dialogue with a priest. The attitude of confession — telling all — is useful. *I confess to myself . . . .*

It is also crucial that this review, like all other aspects of spiritual practice, take place on a daily basis. If we do not monitor ourselves regularly on a daily cycle, then things slip by and the transformative dynamic of honesty is lost.

Within the classical spiritual traditions, the institution or the teacher provides the disciplined guidelines within which we do this work. As we move into the 21st century, however, we have mainly thrown away relationships in which we surrender to top-down discipline. This means that we have no option but self-discipline.

## Contemplative Self-Review and Journal-Keeping

In contemplative self-review we sit quietly and allow our mind to remember or replay everything that we have done, thought and felt since the last review.

As our mind runs over the day, it is not the actual events which matter (I had breakfast. I went to work. I did the typing. I saw Jane.). They are superficial. What matters is the quality and the attitude which we brought to each action and event.

This is relevant to the tiniest thing. How did I eat my breakfast — anxiously, calmly, greedily? Oh yes, I notice my anxiety. I was anxious. I am an anxious person. I am shining light upon myself. How did I greet my partner first thing in the morning? Did I notice her? What quality of communication did I share?

This self-questioning is relevant to all aspects of our lives. I was once involved in a friend's very exciting financial success after months of difficult selling and negotiating. The result was wonderful and from an everyday perspective the event was fabulous. But when we contemplated the success in self-review it was very different. It was sobering to recognise the unpleasant atmosphere of the transaction and the emotions at the final signing. This realisation did not detract from the grounded success of the deal, but it did mean that we had things to learn about attitude and behaviour for similar situations in the future.

This business of attitude rather than action needs careful attention. I remember the terrible moment in my own meditation when I contemplated how I would judge my life if I were to die that second. I looked back at the various things that I had done: school, work, retreats, university, books, organisations, relationships . . . . The actions and products began to evaporate and I was left only with a sense of the moods and attitudes that I was leaving behind. I looked back and I saw none of my actions. I saw only the texture and energy of my attitudes and moods. I leave behind me the echo of my moods. They will endure. That is a sobering epitaph for those of us who are focused only on product and achievement.

This is the key, though, to effective self-reflection. What is our mood? What is our psychological state? What use is it, for example, if we help someone but we do so with an egoistic attitude? What use is it if we agree to do something, but our attitude is resentful?

Being honest about our 'stuff' is no great thing, you might protest. Perhaps. But if we shine the light of our awareness onto our petty, unpleasant and egoistic attitudes regularly, day after day, something transformative begins to happen. The simple act of becoming aware of an attitude may in itself transform it; that layer of the onion simply falls away. I know a woman who noticed that she handed over her daughter's pocket money begrudgingly. Noticing it was enough to change her behaviour and attitude. Shine a light on a shadow and it may evaporate. Notice that a tree is about to fall on you and you move.

The techniques are simple. Every day take some quiet time. Either close your eyes and review the previous twenty-four hours, or write about them in a diary. Be honest and be open. Many of us integrate the self-review into regular meditation. I will write more about this further on in the book.

## Breath and Vipassana

The other major technique for self-monitoring is the use of breath. This is taught in many traditions, but is most well known in the Buddhist Vipassana discipline. In this tradition the students simply sit, breathe and observe their internal state and reactions. Sitting and breathing, doing nothing else except observing yourself sitting and breathing, you begin to notice areas of tension in the body. You notice the tendency for the rhythm of your breathing to become jagged and irregular. Sitting for a longer period of time, you also begin to experience waves of irritation, pain and disturbance; these occur in the form of physical and emotional feelings and uncontrollable thoughts.

If you sit for a long period of time, holding your breath to a regular rhythm, inevitably you become painfully aware of your wounds, resistances and shields. This happens because psychological traumas, both the subtle ones and the more obvious ones, do not exist simply in the mind but anchor themselves into the physical body. Sooner or later, when you spend long periods in rhythmic breath, the physical tensions become obvious. For some people, just the idea of sitting quiet and still for an hour is enough to have them jumping out of their skin.

There are two basic forms of breathing that are widely taught. The essence of both of them is to keep on breathing and to hold an attitude of detachment. Whatever else is going in our body or psyche, we can still control our breath and focus. We notice the irritation or obsessive thoughts, but we stay detached; we do not identify with them, we do not buy into them.

The first technique is the flow of continuous breath. In continuous breath there is no break between inhalation and exhalation and the next inhalation. They all flow smoothly into each other. To achieve this the breathing needs to be calm and relaxed. Many people breathe naturally like this when they are relaxed.

The other form of breathing is one in which there is a

distinct pause between in-breath and out-breath, and between out-breath and in-breath. The in-breath and out-breath also have a distinct rhythm. There are many different rhythms taught, but the most common is the 7-1-7-1. We count up to seven on the in-breath. Pause for one count. Count up to seven on the out-breath. Pause for one count. Count up to seven on the in-breath. And so on.

For both techniques the breath can be focused in various places: high in the chest, in the middle at the diaphragm or in the abdomen; or in the whole chest area. Using this technique you can feel where there is tension and anxiety, and where to direct and hold the breath.

This mode of self-monitoring is different from contem-

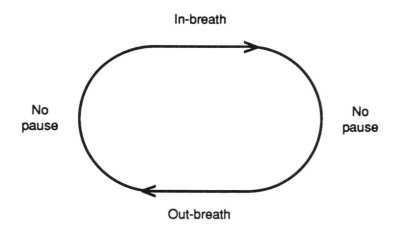

**Continuous breath**

plative review or journal-keeping in that it does not specifically name the attitudinal and behavioural patterns that are causing the distress. It feels them as uncomfortable — sometimes traumatically painful — blockages of energy in the body. In the jargon of this approach, we 'breathe through' the tensions. This means that by holding a clear attitude of detached observation and by holding the discipline of the rhythmic breath, the flow of the breath — under centred and detached control — releases and transforms the painful knot of energy. It is difficult to appreciate the beauty of breathing through one's pain unless you have actually experienced it. But it is a standard mode of transformation across the world. Its more elaborate variations are taught in

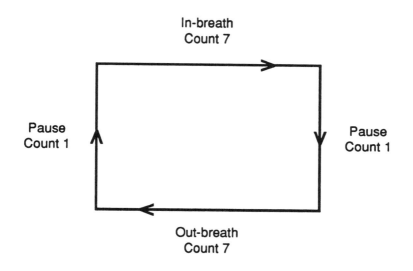

**Counted breath**

the different schools of asana yoga; and it is the basis for such modern therapies as rebirthing and holotropic breathing.

You can imagine, I am sure, the power of Vipassana when practised over many years for extended periods.

Essentially the technique is simple. Sit down and watch your breath. Breathe through the tensions.

## The Inner Healer and Therapist

Breathing through our stuff, combined with contemplative self-reflection, is obviously very powerful and useful. It is the basis of much meditation work. Although sooner or later every wound and shield will become apparent, there are many patterns which are too deep-rooted and painful to be transformed with ease. The discomfort of dealing with them will often motivate us to try to avoid them. The most usual avoidance pattern is to stop doing daily self-reflection.

Simply recognising that we will try to escape the discomfort is useful and we can use self-discipline to see us through the rocky period. But there is another strategy that people are finding increasingly helpful. In this strategy, when we encounter those parts of ourself that are deeply wounded and resistant, we begin an internal conversation with them. We act as a healing therapist to our own wounded self.

The first step in being our own therapist is to adopt an attitude of listening and to be ready to accept our wounded aspects. We need to understand these parts of ourself and we need to discover what they require in order to melt, transform and heal.

We may, for example, in self-reflection notice a chattering spoilt child within ourself who acts disruptively when not receiving attention. Having noticed this pattern one of our options, of course, is simply to stop the child and change its behaviour. But it might be more appropriate to work with the cause and not just the symptom, for even if the surface behaviour changes, the underlying cause may remain and surface again in some other form.

All this is fairly obvious psychology for many people and anyone who has a little knowledge of psychotherapy will recognise these basic truths. This is one of the reasons why I recommend that everyone starting meditation or a spiritual practice spend some time becoming familiar with therapy and counselling — through either receiving therapy or counselling, or training in them, or at least reading some books which describe the therapeutic and counselling process. It can only do us good. Most importantly, having learnt something of these techniques, we can take them into the privacy of our own transformative process and use them in inner dialogue.

The only reasons for not learning about this area are fear and pride — and fear and pride are only patterns ready for transformation.

D.H. Lawrence's poem 'Healing' is helpful.

*I am not a mechanism, an assembly of various sections.*
*And it is not because the mechanism is working wrongly,*
*that I am ill.*
*I am ill because of wounds to the soul, to the deep*
*emotional self*
*and the wounds to the soul take a long, long time,*
*only time can help*
*and patience, and a certain difficult repentance,*
*long, difficult repentance, realisation of life's mistakes,*
*and the freeing oneself*
*from the endless repetition of the mistake*
*which mankind at large has chosen to sanctify.*

## Integrity

This self-reflection is part of the daily rhythm of all spiritual disciplines and gives us the integrity of self-watchfulness and the power of realistic humility.

People who have been doing this kind of self-honesty practice for years actually get to enjoy what may appear at first glance to be an unpleasant process. There is little that is more satisfying than to catch hold of one our patterns, understand it and then change it. It is also amusing to realise how cunning the mind and psyche are at denying the truth and attempting to ignore our psychological reality.

## The Royal Art — Exploring the Soul

I have devoted much attention to the wounds, problems and challenges of our everyday personality and to its onion-layered defences and attitudes. But also present within us is our core self, our soul. We want to know it better and to bring it more fully into our life. Within the spiritual traditions, which teach about the purpose and nature of the core self, there is general agreement that to achieve the full presence of the core self, to have it incarnate fully — to have it come in for a complete landing — is, in fact, the summation and spiritual conclusion of the human process. This is the true mystical marriage of the Christian mystics and Sufis; it is the liberation of the East; it is the reintegration of the western magical traditions; it is the dross turned fully to gold of the true alchemical teachings. The social-psychological self is so transformed, and the core self is so present, that the two marry. We then live in a state of complete fulfilment, of wisdom, knowing and unconditional love.

But we can only get on with this Great Work or the Royal Art, if we can identify the soul in the first place. Identifying it and bringing it more fully into our awareness is much more subtle and difficult than self-reflection on our attitudes and behaviour. This is because the core self is not dramatically obvious. If it were dramatically obvious then there would not be any argument in the first place as to whether it even exists. The great mystic may know all about it; but the materialistic intellectual may think that any idea of the soul is rubbish.

For us, the challenge is to make the subtle more obvious.

The core self is an energy presence and a consciousness different from our everyday experience. Unique for each of us, it is the dynamic organising principle of our psyche, holding our direction together in the midst of all the defences, wounds and patterns.

An image that I often use is that of the core self being like a feather and the everyday social-psychological self being like water. The core self floats on the surface of the water, subtle and very light. It needs the weight of experience and the thinning of the water before it can begin gently to sink and be fully present. It is like the halo around the moon. It is like an overlighting ethereal consciousness who knows who we are, where we have been and where we are going and guides us invisibly through our life.

Many mystics — and we are all potential mystics — have a full experience of this core self. The personality vibrations slow down, the mind opens and the consciousness and brain have a full experience of the core self. The feather strokes the brain cells and the mystic experiences bliss and ecstasy.

Many people never have this kind of experience, but they do have other experiences which give clues and sometimes clear openings to the core self. It is necessary to look at these experiences to remind us just how we are in touch with our soul.


## The Moral Imperative

Earlier I wrote about the natural sense of justice and morality that we possess, as children and as adults. Some of this sense comes from having internalised the attitudes of parents and other authority figures, but much of it also comes from an inherent instinct and knowledge. It is worth asking ourselves where this inherent instinct, which we all have, comes from. It seems to me that there can only be one answer, which is that there is an inner aspect of ourselves which is in tune with natural justice and morality. Our sense of a moral imperative derives surely from our core self.

It is very powerful, isn't it, to notice our own sense of morality and to know that its source is our own core self? I want to wave a flag at those people who think they never have soul contact. Look! We have it all the time.

It is good to remember those occasions when the injustice of a situation has overwhelmed us and called forth our deepest compassion. In those moments we experience clearly our own soul.

It is worth reinforcing and exploring this awareness of our innate morality and inner direction. The easiest way to do this is in a quiet meditative or contemplative state. We can then contemplate the following kinds of questions: How do I know right and wrong? How do I know that what I did in that situation was wrong and inappropriate? What is good? What is evil? Where does my sense of discrimination come from? Where do I, the observer, get these ideas of what would be correct and appropriate behaviour? From where do I get my sense of justice and morality?

## The Inner Self Has a Different Atmosphere

Another clear indication of our core self is its subtle but powerful atmosphere — if only we bother to take notice of it. There are some very clear and everyday examples.

If we sit quiet and calm for a while, there is a distinct change in the atmosphere and vibration of our body and personality. This change in vibration is so distinct that it can be scientifically measured in the frequency of the waves transmitted by the brain. Equally, if someone sits quietly in one place regularly, then that place itself will absorb the atmosphere radiated by the silent person. This is absolutely tangible in, for example, libraries and places of worship and meditation. This happens because the soul has its own vibration which can be distinctly felt provided we go quiet enough to let it through, and quiet enough to notice it.

Just as our personality has vibrations which are radiated into the environment, so does our core self. It is worth sitting quietly to observe its resonance and feeling. This, in one way, is the purpose of meditation: to sit quietly and to become familiar with the silent radiation of the inner being. It is impossible to do this if our awareness is contained within the 'noise' of a busy personality with all its physical feelings, emotions and thoughts. So it is necessary to get the personality vibrations calm. Once they are calm, we can experience that different aspect of ourselves. Without stress, relaxed and contemplative, we begin to get a sense of this more subtle inner person. All the many different forms of stress control, meditation and yoga take the practitioner into a state where they can feel this inner person. For many people it is enough simply to take twenty minutes a day to sit quietly, breathe calmly and wait patiently for the inner peace which belongs to the core self — an inner peace which may sometimes explode into a full-blown altered state of consciousness.

## Altered States of Consciousness

Most people, at one time or another, experience altered states of consciousness or heightened awareness. According to a Gallup opinion poll conducted a few years ago, over fifty per cent of people report having had at least one experience of another presence or power.

In fact, I believe that we frequently have these experiences but do not bother to pause and properly notice them. We have a sense of something, but it is not discernible by the usual five physical senses. Often we have this experience when we are moved by something of beauty, such as landscape, music or a beautiful action. Instead of a gasp of wonder at the beauty, there is a longer experience of wonderment. It is worth re-creating these experiences, either in action or imagination, and noticing everything that is happening within us. The physical sensations, the emotion, the idea, the mood and inspiration may all be indications of how we feel the presence of our own soul.

Equally, many people have a heightened experience of their core self when they are fully engaged in a situation or encountering an image that calls forth their compassion. For many years I worked with adults and teenagers with special needs. Particularly when working with those with severe physical disabilities I found that the situation evoked from me a core sensitivity and presence.

Like a trekker in the wilderness, we need to stalk our core self. It is not so much that the experiences seem so wonderful and phenomenal when they are happening. But, if we remember and contemplate them carefully, they stand out in comparison to our other experiences and awarenesses. They leave a quiet echo or gentle glow.

Some spiritual and psychotherapeutic schools teach specific visualisation and meditation exercises which deliberately bring the student into contact with the core self. In these exercises the core self is perceived through an image. One of the most famous of these guided meditations involves the student, relaxed and contemplative, in leaving a beautiful meadow, walking up a high mountain and then, at the peak, entering a white temple. In the temple there is a fountain at which we drink and then a beautiful being appears. We can talk to this being and ask her/him questions. We then leave the temple and come back down the mountain to the meadow.

Another famous meditation involves contemplating a being who, for us, is perfect and wonderful. With a clear sense of this being, we then place her/him in our heart and contemplate the experience.

There is also the mystical technique which uses affirmations. For example we may dare to say to ourself: 'I am Spirit' or 'I am the Christ Within', until finally the statement actually rings true and authentic. The fact that such an affirmation can ring true is not because of ignorant or egoistic delusion, but because there is genuinely something in each of us which is part of cosmic consciousness. We absorb the experience and then in self-review we can contemplate whether we were deluded or hitting a genuinely authentic note which gives us a deeper sense of our core self.

## Purity and Purification

A brief word on purity in spiritual practice is needed. The kinds of question that are frequently asked concern diet and vegetarianism, money and charity, relationships and sex, possessions and poverty. Throughout the ages different schools and traditions have laid down different guidelines concerning all these things, and unpleasant arguments can happen between proponents of the different approaches. Worse than the arguments are the psychological traps in which people find themselves.

The spiritual path is about achieving liberation of the soul once we have become fully at one with it. One aspect of this liberation is the paradox of complete surrender to the sacred or inner life whilst also taking full responsibility for ourself. We are free, therefore, to make these decisions for ourself.

Different disciplines and forms of purification work for us at different times. It is worth experimenting and discovering that which helps our spiritual unfoldment, understanding that what works today may not be relevant tomorrow. Providing that whatever we do is monitored on a daily basis, then we will have a clear sense of what is appropriate. Careful self-review will indicate soon enough if a vegetarian diet is needed or even a fast. Equally in self-review we can notice easily enough if we have the wrong attitude to money or possessions. All we need is a watchful eye, scanning the different aspects of our life and always open to appropriate change and action.

# Chapter Six

# Alignment With the Sacred

## 'God'

The sacred, the divine, the multidimensional, the magical, is around us and within us. As children we often experience this other reality, but the immediacy of physical, psychological and social existence penetrates our vulnerability and we build up defensive — and successful — personas for coping with it. As this happens we lose our openings of communication with the other, inner world. We close down, and create and thicken our defences.

Later, for one reason or another, we begin to recall this inner world and its sacred beauty. We begin to sense that there is some form of underlying and transcendent connection between everything. We may call this Spirit or God. It is useful to understand that 'God' is shorthand for an indescribable reality which is experienced in various ways in different traditions and individuals. For some people it is a very personal experience; others are more detached. Generally we tend to project onto 'God' ideas that suit our society. A patriarchal society has a patriarchal God.

Some spiritual traditions, such as Buddhism, recognise this tendency to appropriate, exploit and manipulate the idea of God. These traditions recognise that defining God is a matter of where we place our attention and how we attune our perception.

In the mystical tradition of Judaism there is a helpful

map of inner realities called the Kabbalistic Tree of Life. On this tree are ten great spheres, each of them representing an aspect of the sacred or an expression of God. The lowest sphere represents the Earth and the highest sphere represents the radiance of pure cosmic consciousness and the Source of all that is manifest. Above this highest sphere, however, there are three further half circles, each higher than the previous one, sitting like hats on top of each other. The first of these crescents represents *The Unknowable*. The second represents *The Absolutely Unknowable*. The third and highest is named *The Absolutely Completely Unknowable*.

The Tibetan teacher Djwahl Khul, well known through the many books of Alice Bailey, most of the time studiously avoids the word *God*, preferring to use the phrase *All That Is*. And J.G. Bennet, who taught and initiated people into a mystic way called *Subud*, once had a student who upon entry into the order refused to go along with a pledge to *God*. Bennet's students were dismayed, but Bennet looked at the rebel and asked, 'How about a pledge to *Cosmic Electricity*?' The rebel nodded that he could accept such a notion and Bennet flowed ahead with the entrance.

This digression about God underlines a crucial point about true spiritual practice. In it, as private individuals, we are free to explore what God is or is not, or whether we even choose to relate to the concept at all. What is central is that there is an inner world and that there is a sacred quality to all life. In spiritual practice we explore these worlds, free of preconceptions, open to the unknown.

Some people may say that they are incapable, perhaps even unworthy, of experiencing the sacred. This is not possible. No person, unless deprived by terrible injustice, lives without tasting the experience.

We feel it in beautiful landscape; sometimes we experience it when looking at a child or holding something beautiful. It may gently stroke our consciousness, like the touch of a feather. At some point in our life, the magic quality of the inner world has touched us. Only remember and notice it.

In spiritual practice, on an ongoing daily basis, we deliberately do certain things to cut through our psychological defences and to bring us into communication and communion with this inner reality. There are many different techniques and approaches — spiritual technologies — but the purpose of all of them is to bring the sacred and the divine into our *conscious* awareness, and to repeat the experience so often that it fuses into our daily consciousness.


## Abandon, Devotion and Contemplation

It is one of the joys of human culture that there are so many different approaches to God or Spirit — but it is also a challenge. It is a challenge because one of the more terrrible problems of humanity is that people are often intolerant of spiritual paths different from their own. I am not just thinking here of the obvious theological conflicts between religions and belief systems. I am also thinking of the very different *styles* of spiritual approach. These differences in style can provoke terrible prejudice and are perhaps more of a problem than the theological and intellectual divisions. Theological conflicts are easily identified, but those between styles can exist within the same belief system and are more insidious. There seem to me to be three basic styles which appear to conflict and create trouble between their practitioners. These styles are:
- Mystical abandon
- Devotional aspiration
- Contemplation

Imagine, for example, a devotional seeker who loves intense prayer and a person who meets Spirit by dancing in abandon. The one may be deeply alienated by the style of the other. In the same way, a seeker who enjoys the more contemplative approach may be highly judgemental of both the devotee and the dancer. In fact, the three styles need not be mutually exclusive. It is worth regularly monitoring ourselves and asking which of the three styles is our predominant way; then asking whether it is appropriate to try one of the others; and making certain we melt any prejudices against them.

In the section after next I will try to identify many of the different techniques. This can be useful not only because it helps us to avoid conflict, but also because it expands the range of approaches that we ourselves can use. It may be time for many of us to try completely new ways.

## Open Yet Focused

At the core of all the different styles and techniques, however, there is a common element: a willingness to allow our consciousness access to the sacred, a *willingness to surrender to the sacred*. This surrender does not mean losing control. It means liberating our consciousness from the constraints that prevent our natural interplay with the divine.

As children we are allowed to be open to the imaginative world of impressions. We have to give ourselves that freedom again. We need that psychic freedom in order to explore the whole cosmic world which exists within and beyond what we perceive with our usual five senses.

But we need to be clear. We free our perception and imagination to be in the state they were in when we were children; but we do it as adults. Many of us, as we re-approach the inner world, are frightened that we shall not be able to differentiate between the imaginary and the real. The fear is that we may lose ourself, not in the inner world of the sacred, but in the imaginations of our own wounded or undisciplined psyche. It is useful if this fear transforms into sensible cautiousness and, taking notice of it, we keep our B-S antennae alert and scanning. It is not useful if this fear freezes and traps our psyche. What we need is to allow one part of our psyche free rein and encouragement to explore the inner worlds, whilst at the same time we are also focused, watchful and discriminating.

This may seem contradictory: to be open yet focused. It is not a contradiction. It is simply the use of two of our faculties at the same time. A radar dish, or an electronic telescope, is open and receptive — yet it is also focused. There are, of course, times when it is appropriate simply to abandon ourselves to the sacred. And to use our discrimination afterwards to assess and to integrate.

At the core, then, of all the spiritual practices that seek consciousness of the divine is this focused openness. The real issue for each of us is to find the method of focused openness, of spiritual approach, that suits and serves our own unique identity.


## More Time and Discipline

Whichever tradition or style we choose, it will demand time and self-discipline. Spiritual exploration requires conscious *effort.* It is this effort which allows the seeker to hold the attitude of open focus. Without effort, self-discipline and concentration, the focus melts away. It does not matter which spiritual technique we use, they all require attention. There is no technique which works casually. If there were, everyone would be doing it, there would be a universal religion and this would be heaven.

When a Sufi mystic of the whirling dervish tradition spins in the great ceremonial dances, it is not the action of the spin itself that creates the mystic awareness. The mystic awareness comes about because the dervish, within the spin, or as the spin, is focused on God. Equally in the wonderful flows of energy that occur in sacred and circle dancing, the music and the movement do indeed carry a divine resonance, but to be open to it the dancer must be focused and disciplined within the steps and rhythm of the dance. It is the willingness to give attention and to be open to the divine which allows the communion.

Dance with a closed inner eye, with the doors of perception firmly closed, and there will be no relationship with the inner world. Equally, there will be no relationship with the inner world without the discipline of focus and awareness.

This business of being attentive is another of our beautiful human paradoxes. We need to be disciplined and focused in order to hold our consciousness open. We are strong in order to surrender. When eastern meditation paths were being introduced to the west in the first half of this century, many of the most well-known teachers found it necessary to teach their students the art of *concentration* first before teaching the actual meditation. In order to meditate — in order to have the consciousness still and open — the mind needs first to learn the discipline of attentiveness. In some of the Zen traditions the teacher never says anything more to his students than: *Attention!* (Occasionally he may hit them as well.)

Discipline and concentration is found in its most passionate form in those seekers who approach the divine through fiery and devotional prayer. Their body language of kneeling, bowed bodies, hands held together, fingers pointing upwards, reflects the concentration of the purposeful approach to cosmic consciousness. These prayerful mystics are seeking, like a rocket thrust up into heaven, direct communion with the Most High and are prepared to subject their bodies and personalities to humble ignominy in order to achieve it. I have a particular fondness for this path because it cuts quickly through a lot of personal rubbish. It can be damaging if repressed areas of the psyche are never recovered to be nurtured and healed, but as a path of direct contact it can hardly be equalled. The trick though, yet again, is that within the fervour and fiery concentration, the mind needs to be open and scanning for the divine. The bliss of divine contact does not come from introvert focus, but from openness.

## The Mystic Supermarket

In one form or another we have to spend some time every day exploring and attuning to Spirit — contemplating it, abandoning ourselves to it, aspiring to it. So the question is: What practice are you going to adopt?

The best that I can do here is to list several of the different approaches. The reader may be unhappy that I am not giving techniques in greater detail, but that was never the purpose of this short book. I want to provide a stimulating and encouraging psychological framework for understanding spiritual practice. Readers will have to research the practices for themselves, then actually try them to get a sense of what is appropriate and useful. Careful experimentation works. In the final chapter I will attempt to give some helpful advice about picking and choosing.

What I suggest is that at the very beginning of this process you take some time to review the moments in your life that have been peak experiences and times when you have come into contact with the sacred. Do not censor yourself and do not be surprised at what comes to mind. You may realise that you have these experiences every time you look at the night sky or a beautiful sunset. Certain landscapes may have moved you. Sex. Childbirth and children. Compassion and kindness. A teacher or teaching. A work of art or dance or performance. A prayer or meditation. A sacred place. Any one of these may have moved you into a transcendent consciousness. It may have lasted only a few seconds or it may recur so frequently, like a response to the night sky or sunset, that you consider it not worth noticing.

The key is that we must notice these things and, having noticed, work to turn the volume up and lengthen the experience. We then have two choices. We can deliberately repeat the actual circumstances, if that is practically possible, or we can re-create them in our meditation and contemplation. The art here lies in remembering the full dynamic of the occurrence. Let us examine a practical example by considering the sunset experience.

Many people, watching the extraordinary colours and light of a sunset, have a distinct experience of the sacred aspect of life. Its beauty is so fantastic and its atmosphere so transcendent that we directly meet Spirit. We gasp, or swoon into an altered awareness, or observe and allow ourselves to be transported. Later, sitting quietly and meditatively, we can begin to build up the same experience, but without the sunset itself. The trick is to imagine that we are watching the sunset again and, within the privacy of our own psyche, to allow that memory to trigger the feelings that went with it. This technique requires complete relaxation and openness. We recall all the elements that were evoked by the sunset: the sensation in the body, the change in atmosphere, the feeling around the eyes, the sense of joy or transcendence. The point here is to take the seed of our actual experience, to appreciate and fully explore this seed, and then to let it grow.

Providing you are relaxed and meditative, it is possible to re-create that mystic sense and experience very easily, but it is likely that you will only be able to hold it for a few moments. In spiritual practice we take the seed of these few moments and by carefully working with it, day by day, year after year, we become accustomed to being in the transcendent experience. After a while we can sit comfortably in this state of being, not just for a few seconds but for long periods — and then we gradually come to see what our consciousness wants to explore next, what further aspects of the divine we are drawn to contemplate and absorb. All this, of course, can be part of a regular meditation practice.

It is very useful, if you are setting off on the path, to sit down with a piece of paper and jot down those moments and experiences that brought you in contact with the magic or inner peace of life. Having listed the experiences, then carefully note exactly what it felt like for you. Remember it all in detail and bring fully into your awareness that this is where your exploration of the sacred begins. It does not begin outside yourself in a practice given to you by others. It begins in the privacy of your own experience with the magic of life. This integral part of yourself needs clear recognition and strengthening.

Sitting in silence — meditation — is the major technique worldwide for exploring the inner self and the inner universe. Since the beginning of recorded history women and men have withdrawn from everyday social life into the quiet of retreat, and sitting in silence have opened themselves to the multidimensional and the divine. Meditation practices can also be easily integrated into everyday life and many people, perhaps hundreds of thousands, do this.

*First Steps* is not a meditation book, but there is a point that I would like to emphasise. This is basically the agony and the ecstasy of meditation. The ecstasy is the deep relaxation, calm and communion with the sacred. The agony is that it is difficult to start a meditation practice. It is easy to keep it going for a few days at first, but then the layers of wound and defence begin to surface in our consciousness. We experience acute discomfort, our mind begins a lunatic psychobabble and endless itches and fidgets torture us. Just sensing that this will happen is enough to stop most people getting into a meditation practice. All kinds of wonderful excuses and rationalisations will appear that prevent it. The most usual is that I have too much work — either at home or at the office — and I do not have the time or space. It takes between one and three months to get beyond this and to settle into a comfortable rhythm. Meditation is like any craft, art or profession. It is the practice that brings expertise, excellence and ease. Even then, over the years, the internal madness will still surface regularly. This is normal and is part of the the process of how we come to know and transform ourselves.

*Prayer*

In prayer, using emotional and mental will, we simply cut through our illusions and onion layers of defence, and move straight into communication with the sacred, with God. If we think of the most famous of all the Christian prayers, it begins *Our Father, who art in Heaven* .... Here, with the very first words, we are in direct communication with the divine parent. There need be no pause, as in meditation, for the internal psychobabble to die down and physical tension to be released. The oldest known prayer, the Sanskrit *Gayatri*, begins in a similar mode: *O Thou who givest sustenance to the universe, from whom all things proceed* .... The communication is direct.

The major difference between prayer and meditation is that, whilst meditation requires the personality vibration to be passive, prayer actually harnesses the personality. In prayer, our feelings and thoughts are deliberately turned to focus, with desire and aspiration, on the divine.

Prayer can also become meditation and meditation can become prayer. Having addressed the divine with the fiery aspiration of prayer, it is easier to enter into quiet contemplation. Equally we may begin with quiet contemplation before engaging in direct communication with Spirit. In a sense this is academic and many mystics will say there is no difference between prayer and meditation because, anyway, all life is prayer and meditation.

*Landscape and Nature*

There is something deep in the physical or cellular make-up of humanity that allows us to experience the divine through nature. It is as if there is some primitive memory within us of a pure and natural relationship with our environment. This relationship is not scarred or warped by human pain — there are no layers of defence or wound intervening — but has such an astonishing directness that it can take our breath away and make us swoon into bliss.

Wordsworth:

> *I have felt*
> *A presence that disturbs me with the joy*
> *Of elevated thoughts; a sense sublime*
> *Of something far more deeply interfused,*
> *Whose dwelling is the light of setting suns,*
> *And the round ocean and the living air,*
> *And the blue sky, and in the mind of man.*

If landscape and nature bring us into communion with the divine, then it is intelligent not to deny ourselves its grace. Equally, when in it, it is intelligent to be conscious rather than casual about its transcendent qualities. Then, back in the city or in the office, we can draw on the memory, re-create the experience and come genuinely back into contact with the sacred.

The use of landscape and nature to awaken our spirit is naturally a worldwide phenomenon. It is used, however, much more self-consciously for spiritual awakening by tribal societies with an indigenous shamanistic tradition. Nowadays there are many nature and wilderness workshops available to westerners who need to taste that type of experience. This is from an Eskimo woman shaman:

> *The great sea*
> *Has set me adrift*
> *It moves me*
> *As the weed in a great river*

*Earth and the great weather*
*Move me*
*Have carried me away*
*And move my inwards parts with joy.*


*Housework and Daily Yoga*

The goal is to perform every action with awareness of the Self and of the sacred. This is what the best spiritual communities attempt to teach: awareness of the divine and love in everyday actions. But it is difficult to remain in such a state continuously. It is helpful, therefore, to select particular areas of our daily life to become times for awareness.

When I awake in the morning, I immediately begin to hold awareness. *Here I am, in my body, present, breathing.* I hold it for a while. Then I walk to the bathroom and lose it. I have a habit, however, of reawakening when I brush my teeth. I brush my teeth with awareness. I used to do it harshly and fast. I then lose awareness again until I am sitting for my morning meditation. I reawaken if I am travelling and caught in a traffic jam. I remember my breath and I remember that all life is sacred; I breathe this awareness through my body. Then the traffic flows and I begin to forget again. I am brilliant at remembering when I find myself in the wrong queue at the post office, especially when the whole place is beginning to fill with an atmosphere of deadly impatience. I breathe and see the sacred in everything. I was sharing this with a group once and the man sitting opposite asked whether I knew what his job was. I said that I did not and he told me that he worked behind the counter at a post office. 'It's worse,' he said, 'on my side.' I now try to colour my awareness with compassion when in these infernos.

Some people use a particular piece of housework as a time to tune into the divine. One woman I know always washes the dishes with divine awareness; a man I know refuses to get a dishwasher. Another woman taught me how to wash and clean the lavatory with love. This approach can be used in our worklives. We can find ways of experiencing our workplaces as sacred spaces. As we go into and sit through endless meetings, we can quietly attune to and greet the inner selves of all those who are there.

Each of us can find our own times to practise this awareness. In many ways it is very useful to choose the things that we most dislike doing and to transform them into points of divine focus. This does not mean disengaging into some other-wordly state; it means being fully present. Again, when this is done daily, the momentum can be powerful and of great service.

There is a visualisation exercise I developed for insight into spiritual ecology. In this exercise we take our awareness to some part of our home which we know is filthy. Behind the oven or fridge is often a good place to start. We focus on the grease and grime. We then go into a particular speck of grime and into one of its molecules, then an atom. In visualising the atom in the greasy grime, we begin to attune to the life and electricity in the atom. We come into communion with the sacred energy, dynamic and glowing within it. Then we slowly bring our attention back to the whole filthy area, but still holding our awareness of the sacred.

This is a useful exercise in several ways. In my life it helps me look at and come to terms with physical realities I might otherwise continue to deny or ignore. It helps me see the 'light' in everything. And, finally, it allows me to change my attitude, so that I can actually get on with the job and clean up the dirt. This exercise can be used in many other situations. As always, it is a matter of attention and focus.

In many traditions this ability to be fully present, conscious in every moment and situation, is taught through the practice of walking meditations. We walk and we move, and simultaneously we hold our awareness focused and detached. Focused and detached, but *aware* — we do not walk passively or ignorantly into tree trunks or across busy highways. Holding a meditative focus on the sacred essence of all life, we walk our walk, wash our dishes, live our life.


*Ritual and Ceremony*

In ritual and ceremony we choose certain actions and words, and by doing and saying them with awareness we transform them into spiritually charged events. This method can be used with ordinary everyday actions or it can take the form of much more elaborate ceremonies which, word by word and action by action, symbolically address the sacred.

Brushing our teeth or washing up with awareness can become daily ceremonies. The event becomes an opportunity for spiritual practice and, done daily, builds up power. Ritual and ceremonial consciousness make events sacred. I can kiss thoughtlessly; or, with awareness, I can turn it into a ceremony.

In most spiritual traditions the lighting of a candle, for example, is a moment of alignment with the sacred. Many people light candles ceremonially at home. They do not simply light them for the pleasing glow; they are ceremonially aware of the act of creating fire and flame, and consciously use this as a doorway to sacred awareness.

Many cultures and individuals use blessings to affirm spiritual awareness and to bring that spirituality into an object or event. It can be as simple as taking a few moments' silence before eating, or it can be a whole series of actions, such as those used to bless a new home.

Many people are profoundly affected by religious ceremony — not simply by the significance of the gestures and words, but by the atmosphere generated by them. Again, if this is what touches you, then you need to be aware of it and it would be intelligent to develop it. All the major religious traditions have interesting and moving ceremonies. There are also specific ritual groups which work with the ceremonial approach to the divine, for instance western Freemasons or North American Indian groups. There are books available too that help with creating one's own rituals and ceremonies.

*The Arts*

We have already mentioned dance, but for many people the arts in general create points of access to the sacred. In fact, in many cultures art, dance, drama and prose are only expressions of the sacred. At one time, for example, all theatre was sacred drama.

Finding spirit in the arts can happen both through being a practitioner and through being an appreciative member of the audience. In all the arts — when they are carried out with an open focus on the sacred — many people experience a direct relationship with a divine muse or some magical inspiration. Equally, listening, reading and watching can light the spiritual flames of the heart and mind. The mystic Slovenian sculptor Marko Pogacnik teaches people how to appreciate art by suggesting simply that they look for God in it.This applies equally to music: *listen for the sound of the Sacred*.

*Sacred Movement*

There are also forms of movement which deliberately work to attune the body and consciousness to harmony and the sacred. Currently the most well known of these forms is the eastern practice of Tai Chi, in which the body is led into a flow of movement that resonates with the archetypal flow of the earth and heavens. This form of movement is even more explicitly spiritual in the practice of Chi Qong, in which students are taught to work directly with energy flows.

The West also has its own traditions of sacred movement in the ritual body language of prayer and invocation. These gestures have an ancient history and can be seen, for instance, in the illustrations of classical Egyptian culture. In one such movement the seeker bows to the East and raises her arms to the rising sun, and then slowly lowers them, bringing a blessing down into her body and into the earth. Many folk dances, of course, have a spiritual dimension. Very recently the Five Rhythms work of Gabrielle Roth, for example, has brought certain archetypal rhythms and movements into a modern context.

The movements and postures of hatha yoga, of course, invoke spiritual awareness, as do the breathing exercises of prana yoga. There are also people who experience the sacred through sport. I have heard several athletes describe how they hit a point in their movement when their consciousness enters an altered state and the whole experience becomes ecstatic.

## Sex and Relationship

Sex can also be an occasion for ecstasy. It is really fairly extraordinary, isn't it, the level of pleasure that is embedded in the human nervous system. This level of thrill and pleasure can be harnessed purely for self-gratification, or it can be harnessed to a very careful and caring awareness that fully includes the consciousness and needs of our partner. There are various exercises and techniques, using breath, touch and visual contact, that help individuals and couples harness the erotic and the sexual so as to expand consciousness and more fully experience spiritual love. In the east, in particular, this approach is well known in the teachings of Tantra, but it has also been taught in many other religious cultures. In much mystic poetry our relationship with the divine is expressed through the metaphor of a love affair. The Song of Solomon begins: *I am dark but comely, o ye daughters of Jerusalem . . . .*

## Psychedelic Drugs

All of the different approaches and styles described above have a scientifically observable effect on the body and the brain. In particular they change specific aspects of brain chemistry which allow the mind, as it works through the brain, easier access to the multidimensional. These changes in brain chemistry can also be induced by psychedelic drugs, both naturally occurring and synthesised — e.g. mushrooms, peyote, mescaline, LSD and ecstasy.

In the cultures of many native peoples there exists the honoured practice of taking psychedelic substances in order to induce visions, altered states of consciousness and experiences of the sacred. These native cultures respect, support and embrace such rituals. In modern westernised culture these drug-related practices are not supported. Nevertheless there is a substantial number of western intellectuals and spiritual teachers who have usefully used psychedelic substances, including for example Aldous Huxley, Ram Dass and Jean Houston. An American friend of mine calls these drugs the *avatars* of the plant and mineral realms. (Avatar is the Sanskrit word for a divine being come to spiritually liberate humanity.) These drugs are generally not understood by modern society and many of them are illegal. They have a bad reputation partly because many of them, although originally developed or used for transformational and mystical purposes, have become popularly available and are abused. At the very least you should know about them, for they are — albeit secretly — a portal of change and illumination for many people.

If you ever consider taking any of these drugs, you need to be very certain that you understand their effects and that you have an appropriate support system in case you encounter any psychological difficulties either during the 'trip' or when integrating it afterwards. Never take them casually or without preparation and careful consideration. Usually they will be taken because we have a deep inner sense or instinct that it is appropriate. Most often it is appropriate because there is a threshold of transformation or enlightenment to which we have deep inner resistance. The psychedelic opens the brain and mind consciousness directly to other realities — our resistance is simply ignored or melted through — and we have direct access to transcendental and personal understanding which was previously unavailable. This is an extremely dynamic process and not to be considered by anyone who has the slightest doubt about the suitability of such a practice.

The taking of these substances is obviously *not* a daily

spiritual practice. What is a daily spiritual practice is remembering, working with and integrating the visions, insights and illumination of the experience. There are too many people who have revelations and forget them the next day. The inertia of forgetfulness, the lack of *attention*, is probably the greatest of all human challenges on the spiritual path. Each one of us acts in ways that we know are inappropriate. And each one of us forgets to act in ways that we are know are right. Again, discipline and motivation are needed.

*Gurus and Charisma*

It is also possible to get sacred experience from the presence of another person. This is the essence of having a guru. Through giving receptive focus to the guru, we also give receptive focus to the divine through this individual. The guru need not even be alive. The great religions of Islam, Christianity, Buddhism, Sikkhism and Baha'i, for example, are centred around Gurus so great that their followers tend to see them as absolutely unique expressions of God.

There are, however, challenges and issues concerning an exclusive relationship with a single guru or teacher, especially one who is still alive. Gurus are often like cults in that they attract psychologically weak people who need the safety of an infallible parent. The real problem here is that if someone attacks the guru, then the disciple also feels psychologically threatened and will respond defensively and aggressively. If the disciple is psychologically weak and extremely devoted, then the level of attachment to the guru may become pathological. The guru may also be deluded. Some people say that all gurus are fakes, for the only real guru is the Master within one's own heart.

On the other hand, the relationship with a guru may be perfect.

Some people, such as many Asian Indians, are so accustomed to the idea of everyone needing a guru or master that they might even say that spiritual progress is impossible without one.

In the past I have been dismayed by friends who have become lost in the clutches of a guru. Without exception, though, they have over time — sometimes as long as ten years — emerged from the experience the stronger and the wiser for it. So I have learnt to silence my prejudices. The issue for me is that people may lose their ability to discriminate and to assess their experience. They surrender so completely to receptivity that they lose the discipline of focus and a sense of themselves. You can see, then, that for this reason alone, it is important for people with a guru to keep to their daily practice of *self-reflection,* monitoring who they are and what they are doing. If a guru discourages careful self-reflection, avoid that guru.

In this chapter we have looked at the different ways people expand personal consciousness into cosmic consciousness. This is what all spiritual teachings are about. I apologise for taking such a feast of wonders and daring to compress them all into such a simplistic summary. I hope that the brevity is balanced by it being usefully stimulating.

Even the way in which I have divided the different approaches, although useful for a certain kind of clarification, is false. Prayer becomes meditation. Ordinary actions become meditation become prayer become art become relationship become awareness of the sacred nature of all life. We work to achieve awareness of the true Self and of Spirit in every moment and every action, never-ending, in continuous flow. *How* we do it is a choice that we each make based on what works best for us.

Cosmic consciousness, an expanding awareness of everything that is, communion with the true worlds, is possible. It is possible not just through a tentative thread of awareness, but through an all-pervasive experience in which the sacred is felt in every cell and fibre. This comes through surrender and practice — each of us doing it in our own unique way.

# Chapter Seven

# Actions, Attitude and Service

## The Fire of Idealism

In the practice of self-reflection and the practice of attuning to the sacred, we gain visions and experiences of a world, of a consciousness and of a reality different from that in which we daily live. The sacred world has a quality about it that calms the dynamics of unbridled egoism. The driving need to survive, to compete and to win, retreats in the face of the sense of the true Self and the sacred nature of all life.

The challenge, then, is to remain true to that sense of the Self.

Once we have begun to feel the power of the Self and the sacred, there is a natural drive to fulfil it and to embody it in our whole lives. That instinct which we had as children, that there should be a world of justice and right behaviour, reawakens. Perhaps some of us have managed to hold on to our early sense of natural justice; if that is so, then our new encounters with the inner world will reinforce and empower our awareness and activity. We also learn that there is nowhere for this process to begin except in ourselves.

It seems to me that there exists a natural instinct to surrender to the vision and sense of the Self. I have watched many people who do indeed have a clear sense of their Self but who do nothing to surrender to it in their daily lives.

Without exception these people are wounded by a deep personal dissatisfaction — although their pain may be hidden under veils of psychological defence.

There are other people who surrender with such willingness to the moral imperatives of the Self that their personal sacrifices to the general good can shock and inspire us with their courage and lack of self-interest.

For the sake of ease let us call all behaviour that is dedicated to achieving a moral, just and loving world *service*. Our instinct for service derives, I believe, from an uncontrollable inner desire to bring into tangible manifestation all that we know to be just and beautiful of the true inner world. This is a great passion. It is also a dangerous passion, for most of us prefer safe lives. Caught in the realities of mortgage payments and family commitments, ensnared in the illusions of status and social survival, we find the idea of surrender to the passion of service threatening.

Yet we have no choice except to surrender — each in our own appropriate way — to this passion of service. Our lack of choice derives not only from the moral imperative of our soul. It also derives from the reality that service is the physical foundation stone of our spiritual transformation.

## Service as Personal Transformation

The essence of personal transformation is the process by which our core self, our true inner self, comes into full incarnation and expression. Spiritual transformation is our true self coming in for a landing. Many of us forget this or choose to ignore it. We prefer to think that our main work is to expand outwards into ever less earthly awareness. Certainly we have to expand our consciousness, but all the expansion in the world is useless unless it is brought down and expressed through us in our behaviour, actions and attitudes.

We need to be very clear about this. The reason why we need to *express* our Self is not simply because it is a good idea, or because it is of service. The reason is that *only* when our new consciousness is expressed *through* us do we really change. If it does not express through us then it is happening only in our psyche. New awareness — about love or spirit or consciousness or natural justice — has to ground through us and we have to experience that inner 'friction' that happens when we genuinely act it out in body, mind and heart. It is in this process that we transform ourselves. If our changes happen only in our psyche we are wasting time and it is fair to accuse us of narcissism.

To put it in an energetic way: The core self has a different vibration, radiance and consciousness from the everyday psycho-social self. When the core self comes into and expresses through the everyday self, then the everyday self changes its vibration, radiance and consciousness. In this way transformation, integration and true freedom are achieved.

There are many mystics and spiritual idealists who, because their new awareness is not grounded in the physical reality of their actions, are completely out of balance and in many ways dysfunctional.

The energy field of the Self has to flow fully through our whole being right down into what is often today called our cellular awareness. Every cell of the everyday self needs to vibrate and radiate the awareness of the Self. This is spiritual transformation.

Service, then, seen from another perspective, is that behaviour which expresses our core self into the world.

## Power and the Will-to-Good

We cannot, however, simply wait for our core self to send us overwhelming inspirations to service. We could wait for ever. We need to help the process with, in the words of Alice Bailey, a clear *will-to-good*. This will-to-good draws upon our own purposefulness and it also draws upon the power inherent in the divine. Certainly the divine is love and wisdom and enlightenment, but it is also power. This power can be seen in the extraordinary force of creation. This power — to create and to make all things new — is in us. We draw upon it continuously in almost every choice and movement we make. It manifests also in the self-discipline of honest reflection and in the willed focus needed to explore the spiritual world.

This power-to-change and will-to-serve is in all of us. We need to recognise and find it within ourselves. Often it is most easily recognised as *courage* — the rage of our hearts.

## Service as Attitude

Above I suggested that service is 'behaviour that is dedicated to achieving a moral, just and loving world'. This definition is clear, but it is also open to argument as we may disagree about what works towards achieving this kind of world. Let me illustrate: A woman collecting money for starving children is obviously serving. A woman selling perfume in a boutique is not serving. But suppose that the one collecting the money is doing it in a manner that bullies the donors and the one selling the perfume does it with love and attention. Who is then serving? Our definition of service fails and we are once again faced with paradox.

When assessing service we need, therefore, to appreciate the context and the attitude as well as the action itself. To feed the hungry is obviously service. But to do so with love and care is more effective for bringing in the Self and the sacred. In an impersonal way, feeding the hungry redresses the balance of injustice and acts on behalf of the whole of humanity. It is in itself, therefore, service. But when we perform the action with love and attention, our whole body expresses service and the sacred. We ourself transform and, at the same time, the transformatory vibration goes out into the world. To be exact, our transformatory vibration goes out to those with whom we are in relationship: the people with whom we are working and living.

The woman selling perfume may perhaps be selling stuff that has been tested upon animals and which comes from a thoughtless manufacturer; she may also be working in a shop designed to pander to the illusions of a materialistic and sexist culture. The context makes her actions the opposite of service. But if her relationships with her clients and fellow staff are filled with love, attention and care, who knows the alchemy and redemption that can take place? She may quietly be transforming the whole culture of her workplace. It is not for us to judge her. But if we were in her place, we would have to make careful judgements about whether the integrity of our attitude counterbalanced the apparent uselessness of the actual work.

We each of us have to make careful assessments of what we are doing and how we are doing it. Just because we work somewhere that is not explicitly spiritual or service-oriented is no hindrance to service. The issue is how we deal with our transactions and our relationships. I remember a group in which someone was saying that they could never work in a shop because it supported mindless consumerism and there was no possibility of service. Another woman in the group said simply, 'I treat every shopper as if I were a therapist and they were my client. I have a safe and friendly attitude. I love them.'

Whether we work in shops or laboratories, as professional carers or business people, the issue is attitude. What we can do in every single transaction and encounter is give attention and love. This requires discipline, focus and the will-to-good.

## Relationships at Work and at Home

A major challenge for most of us is that our lives are so compartmentalised that we restrict service to one single aspect, rather than integrating it in a more holistic manner. In a village, tribal or religious community, our general attitude and behaviour would be seen by everyone. In our modern culture there is a tendency to have different roles and attitudes for different parts of our life. This makes it easy for us not to notice or simply to get away with lousy behaviour. There are millionaires who are generous charitable donors but are selfish and brutal with their workforces. There are people in the caring professions who are wonderful with their clients, but awful with their families.

To hold one's centre and to have an attitude of service in daily relationships is not easy. The fact that we are involved on a daily basis may seduce us into a familiarity which at best can result in unconsciousness, at worst in contempt. We can become so familiar with people that they may lose any identity of their own and become simply screens for our projections and targets for our unconscious moods and attitudes. If this happens with our working relationships, it happens doubly so in our families and marriages.

It is in these situations, where we spend most of our time, that we need to practise the greatest care. It is easy to come to centre and hold an attitude of service in specially chosen moments or in an environment where the issues of social injustice or need are clear. But it is not easy to do this in the workplace or home.

To be of service to our family and colleagues can be very painful. It is painful because unconsciously we associate these significant people with all the other significant people who wounded us when we were infants and children. In acts of kindness to these people we are, within our unconscious psychological framework, acting kindly to our enemies, those whom we have every reason to resent. It is easier, isn't it, to perform charitable acts for distressed situations a thousand miles away than for distressed partners in the next room. When Jesus spoke of turning the other cheek he was leading us into the practice of courageous acts of kindness.

I am not here trying to lead people into a self-sacrificial mode of life in which emotions that need nurture and healing are repressed by the jackboot of service. I am writing about the courage and discipline to cut through self-pity, through inertia and through obsolete patterns of behaviour to do some good in the world. And I am underlining the fact that to do good is not necessarily an overt act of charity, but is in essence an attitude.

I attempt to keep an attitude of goodwill through all my transactions. I believe that this has to begin at home with those most immediately close to me and then with my colleagues. If we take the idea of ecological responsibility seriously, then the closest living creatures in our environment *are* our family and colleagues; it is to them that we owe the first awareness and acts of service. Practising random acts of kindness is helpful. We have to serve our family, friends and colleagues.

## Family

In our marriage, we can melt our way through many crises if we have a willingness to understand that within our relationship our primary responsibility is to serve each other's spiritual growth. Of course, during a row or stimulated by the cunning ego, this might be wrongly interpreted to mean acts of cruelty or patronising advice: I am your teacher, you spiritual cretin, take this!

More appropriately, supported by quiet and careful self-reflection, it can be very clarifying if our first commitment to each other is spiritual service, rather than mutual gratification or the duration of the relationship.

Placing spiritual growth first may sound dangerous because relationships require reliable commitment if we insecure humans are to grow within them. The crux of the matter is that if we make spiritual service a priority in our relationships, then it has to be underpinned by spiritual practice — by careful self-reflection and by alignment with the sacred. It also has to be underpinned by a grounded awareness of emotional nurture and normal mutual support and respect.

For parents, bringing up children can be all too obviously a service activity. Equally, when we are adults looking after our elderly parents, the service aspect is predominant. But especially in these dependent situations we have to be careful to reflect upon our attitude. Here in the psychodrama of our families are the most poignant and challenging opportunities for service.

Again, as ever, we need to give these areas daily awareness and attention.

## Some Helpful Advice from the Western Mystery Tradition

Because service involves so many real challenges I thought it might be useful to drop in here some advice from the western spiritual tradition. It comes in a wonderful set of phrases and can be applied to most challenging situations. The advice tells us:

> To know.
> To dare.
> To will.
> To be silent.

- To know is to understand and to acknowledge the full dynamics of any situation, including the psychological wounds and the ever-presence of the sacred.
- To dare is to take the risk and have the courage to behave in an aligned and centred manner, whatever the pain involved.
- To will is to keep our power, especially that of our core self, engaged and taking us through the process; to endure and not to collapse.
- To keep silent is to keep quiet those parts of our psyche that protest, deny and resist; the parts that are proud, lazy and neurotic.

To know. To dare. To will. To be silent.

## Appreciating Ourselves

Many of us may also feel guilty because we are not on the frontline of obvious, self-sacrificing service. When we come to examine our attitudes in our family and business transactions, however, we can see that, despite glaring faults, we are genuinely trying to live a life of service. The attempt and the will are there. That is the best that any of us can do.

Social activists often make the accusation that mystics who retreat to mountain tops or religious sanctuaries are avoiding their real responsibilities. Perhaps some of these mystics think that they are leaving everything behind, but true spiritual practice brings no escape. It may seem that in single-mindedly pursuing their own transformation they can cut themselves off from the world, but this is to ignore the interconnection of all life. Through waves of spiritual energy the isolated mystic's transformation and prayers touch and help us all.

We may appear to be isolated units within the human family, but seen with the eyes of inner vision our connections are deep and intimate. The transformation of the mystic on the mountain is also a change within me. The sacrifice of your wounded mood to one of service is also my transformation. We work for each other. Nowhere are we separate from service.

Although we may not be on those frontlines of obvious caring and social action, we can still carry a quiet self-respect. In true service our core self comes in to express fully through our life — on the mountain top, in the kitchen, in the chapel, in the office and factory. This work and awareness are not easy. We fall unconscious, we weaken and we fail. But we try again — and again. Most of us are sincere and genuine in our idealism and motivation. We need to appreciate, love and encourage this aspect of ourselves.

## A Blessing?

Perhaps the easiest way of assessing our life in relation to service is to ask ourself, situation by situation, a simple question:

Is my presence a blessing?

## Chapter Eight

# Continuing Education

## The Pursuit of Wisdom

It is worth giving some attention to the ongoing spiritual education that we need to provide for ourselves.

In classical spiritual traditions both the humblest students and the most elevated priests are encouraged and helped to spend a period every day in the study of sacred wisdom. This is deemed necessary food for the soul. No one is exempt. In monasteries and convents the world over there are libraries full of books of wisdom and also contemplative areas where the residents can walk slowly and meditate on the book of life. Study is not restricted to printed texts, but can mean contemplating particular prayers, or seed thoughts, or sacred pictures, patterns and symbols. Sometimes it can mean studying a particular sound or exploring the sacredness of nature.

Most of us do not live within the supportive structure and culture of a monastic atmosphere, so we need to foster our own habit of study and ongoing education. Great minds are never content with their own level of education. Those of us who do not search for ongoing education are held back by a layer of psychological defence: we do not have the courage to recognise our relative ignorance.

## The Spiritual Supermarket

Many people, however, get confused about what they should be studying and reading.

One of the effects of the global communications revolution and the emergence of the global village is that spiritual teachings that were once inaccessible or secret are now on the shelves of our local shops.

Not so many decades ago, enquirers into the spiritual nature of life would have had few avenues of research open to them. Most seekers would have been limited to what their local church or temple had to offer. Today we need not be restricted to the teachings of the religion and culture into which we were born. All the spiritual traditions and cosmologies are now available to us — and added to them are the insights of the new psychology, the new science and the new ecological approaches.

The nature of the core self, the nature of the inner dimensions, the nature of the sacred, have been written about in tens of thousands of books. There are thousands of different approaches to spiritual reality and spiritual transformation. These approaches are all available to us and present a fantastic educational opportunity.

Purists, however, complain that we live in the midst of a spiritual supermarket. Indeed there can be a real challenge for certain types of shoppers in a supermarket. If we have never visited one before . . . . If we are greedy and have no boundaries . . . . If we do not know how to budget . . . .

The spiritual supermarket requires discrimination and intelligent investigation.

# The Discrimination of the Mature Student

The spiritual supermarket can be overwhelming and I suggest the best way to approach it is as if you were retraining or taking a mature student's degree. Give yourself plenty of time to get to know the field. Do not think that you have to make any instant decisions or an immediate life commitment to a particular path or teacher. Nor think that you are going to get instant enlightenment and wisdom. (Ah, well, maybe . . . .)

It is also worth remembering that there is a general psychological pattern for most of us when we approach a new subject. It can take several months of study before we begin really to understand the scope and context of the subject. So be prepared for disorientation.

And be patient.

Entering a well-stocked metaphysical bookshop, we find ourselves surrounded by thousands of titles — the major religious traditions and their different schools, the teachings of native peoples, the esoteric and wisdom traditions, the oracles and divination, the new psychology, the new science, spiritual ecology, channelling . . . . Read me! Read me! If you don't read me, you won't know the truth! Here are the real secrets! I'll change your life! I am the profound teaching!

If you are entering a shop like this for the first time, give yourself plenty of time to dip and to discriminate. See what actually appeals and what touches your mind, heart, instincts and intuition. Some of these books will touch you so deeply you will be amazed. Some of them will simply turn you off. So make a good relationship with your local spiritual/alternative bookshop.

It is also useful to recognise the style of how you read and study. Some people read several books simultaneously.

Some pursue a single subject for months and years. Others change subjects book by book. Recognising your own study habits will stop you feeling competitive or disempowered when you meet someone with a completely different approach and style.

There is also a large number of courses, workshops and schools available. Unfortunately there is no quality control and naturally some of them are deluded or mediocre. Others are run by saints. If we enrol expecting enlightenment and naively open ourselves to the deluded or mediocre we may have an unpleasant experience, which at least will be a lesson in discrimination for the future.

If, as adults, we commit ourselves to career retraining or returning to formal education, we do so with great care and thought. We research the areas in which we are interested. We taste what they are like before we make long-term plans. We should have the same approach to spiritual education. It has often bemused me how people who have conducted their businesses and careers with intelligence and skill revert to naivety when embarking on their spiritual path. Their skills of research, analysis and decision-making are put to the side as if irrelevant to how they approach their spirituality.

This lack of integration is often due to impatience. It is also often due to a deep inner split between that part of our psyche which has been educated into the mechanistic modern world-view and that part which is attuned to the spiritual and the multidimensional. We internalise many of the attitudes of our parents and teachers, and most of these people would have judged our investigation of the self and the sacred unsympathetically. Thus within ourself we have our own internal judge putting down our involvement in the spiritual search. We therefore switch off and repress this internal judge and at the same time switch off and repress our intelligence and discrimination — whereas when researching our spiritual education, whilst remaining intuitive we should be at our most intelligent and discriminating.

## The Rational Mind

This repression of our rational faculties when we open up to the intuitive and spiritual realms of consciousness is a widespread syndrome. It is even rationalised by some spiritual folk into an active attack on the rational mind as being an enemy of spiritual seeking. This is not true. The intelligence of the rational mind is a crucial ally for the seeker. It serves discrimination and it serves enlightenment. The mind is also the analytical aspect of wisdom and compassion. It is only an enemy when it recycles its thoughts with no self-control or when it is an exclusive devotee of the mechanistic world-view. It might be helpful to recall that for some philosophers the rational mind is proof of the existence of the soul; and some philosophers have identified the rational mind actually as the soul.

One of the most satisfying experiences in the world is when the rational mind is enlightened by intuition and we have an *ah-ha* experience of knowing; or when the rational mind, through its ability to analyse, adds wisdom and insight to intuition.

There are, however, people who have been wounded by the mental aggression of bullying parents and teachers. If you are one of these folk, you will naturally tend to gravitate to spiritual teachings that are not heavy with intellectual content. It is helpful to recognise this dynamic and to enter into a healing process so that the power of the rational mind — of your own rational mind — becomes your friend and ally rather than your enemy.

If we do not work at restoring that balance, then we may become space cadets — a state of mystical ungroundedness that is pleasant for a while but unfruitful in the long term. Worst of all, ungrounded mystics often invoke mental hostility and may re-create the bullying and alienation which wounded them in the first place.

Given all those warnings, further education in the spiritual supermarket is wonderful. The beauty is that we all need help, support and inspiration — and there they are waiting to serve us.

NOTE: There are two guidebooks to the spiritual supermarket which readers may find useful: *The Seeker's Guide,* John Button & William Bloom (eds), Aquarian/Harper. *Chop Wood, Carry Water,* Rick Fields & Co, Tarcher/St Martin's Press.

# Chapter Nine

# The Synthesis

The information is very simple for all of us. Every day, in some way, we self-reflect, we align with the divine and we act in service.

In the pure mystical tradition of the recluse on the mountain or in the monastery, the seeker is in continuous meditation doing all three. Receptively focused on the divine. Breathing through and transforming the inner disturbance and suffering. Radiating the transformed and compassionate consciousness out to the world.

In the invisible interlinking of all life, that one seeker's transformation serves all other lives. No action or attitude is isolated. We have responsibility, in the widest sense, for everything we do.

We each of us have something unique and wonderful to give the world. Every small step we take matters. The slightest transformed pattern or loving self-sacrifice is of service to the whole. The slightest flame of courageous self-honesty works for the self-honesty of all of us. Each illumination helps the illumination of all life. Each act of service is of benefit.

At the same time we need to be realistic. Because we are wounded infants with our defences and patterns, because we live with three billion other similarly wounded infants, because of the whole nature of incarnation and suffering, it is not easy to walk the path of the seeker. We each individually have our own karma, our own history of actions and attitudes which we have to redress and balance. We also live within the historical dynamic of the whole human race. We do not create our life in isolation from the rest of our family or nation or humanity as a whole. We are, so to speak, bound up in the total karma of the human race with its huge history that is both tragic and glorious. We have natural limitations and we cannot achieve perfect spiritual practice — not until we ourselves are perfect.

We also need to notice that there is a rhythm and flow to our lives. At times we need to put in great effort; at other times we need to relax. One period is good for intense self-reflection, whilst another is best for reaching out and active service. There is no perfect right or wrong about our spiritual practice. In any given moment or situation, the dynamics will support or suggest a particular approach. For some of us, silent meditation is a life-long affair; for others it may be dance or relationship. Each of us has our own unique cycle of moods, needs and opportunities. I am counselling that we need to be careful to avoid fixed ideas and rigid plans.

The phrase 'spiritual practice' may sometimes sound harsh. I prefer it to conjure up a sense of learning to flow consciously and blissfully with the cosmic dance of unfoldment. This unfoldment is not strict and regimented. It has all the ebbs, currents, whirlpools, chaos and backflows you would expect from the great river of creation. Our spiritual practice, although disciplined and focused, needs to accept and dance with these unordered but beautiful rhythms, if it is to catch the essential love and grace of the system.

There are workshops, cassettes
and other books by William Bloom.
If you would like to know more about them,
please write to:

*Alternatives,*
*St James's Church,*
*197 Piccadilly,*
*London W1V 9RF*